Quickly Knitted
CLOTHES FOR DOLLS

This book is a revised edition of Paragon book N33, "Quickly Knitted clothes for dolls", originally published by Paragon Art Needlecraft Pty Ltd, Sydney, NSW. The cover of the original book is shown on the front cover. Craft Moods is now the copyright owner and publisher for all Paragon publications.

Edited by: Vicki Moodie.

Copyright: Ray and Vicki Moodie   1997

T0363221

First Revision   January 2002.
Second Revision   May 2011.

ISBN 978-1-876373-76-4

Published by    ®

CRAFT MOODS
PO Box 35
Glass House Mtns QLD 4518
Australia

Tel (07) 53756266

www.craftmoods.com.au

Printed by   Print Approach
                    10 Frawley Ave
                    NARANGBA QLD 4504

                    Tel (07) 38882488

09/20

CONTENTS

ABBREVIATIONS

alt..............	alternate	st(s)...........	stitch(es)
K..............	knit	tog.............	together
P	purl	yfwd..........	yarn forward
psso	pass slip stitch over	yon............	yarn over needle

STITCHES EXPLAINED

garter st.......... knit every row
stst .... stocking stitch (right side knit, wrong side purl)

GENERAL INSTRUCTIONS

All patterns are knitted using 8ply yarn on 4mm knitting needles with a tension of 22½ sts to 10cm measured over stocking stitch. Loose or tight knitters may need to adjust needle size to achieve satisfactory results. Quantity of yarn required is shown for pure wool, less will be required if using acrylic yarn. Each pattern provides instructions suitable for 30cm, 35cm and 40cm high dolls. The "Girl's Outdoor Set" also includes instructions for a 51cm high doll. Where more than one set of figures is given in the instructions, the first refers to the smallest size and those in brackets the medium and larger sizes respectively. Where only one figure is given, it refers to all sizes.

BOY'S OUTDOOR SET

MATERIALS:

Jacket and Beret:
50g (75, 75g) 8ply yarn
Leggings:
75g 8ply yarn
pr 4.00mm knitting needles
70cm of narrow ribbon
45cm of elastic
4 buttons

THE JACKET

BACK

Cast on 30 (34, 38)sts.
Work 5 (7, 7) rows in (K1, P1) rib.
Next row. Rib 2 (1, 3), * increase in next st, rib 4 (5, 5); repeat from * 4 times, increase in next st, rib 2 (2, 4). (36, 40, 44sts)
Work 14 (14, 16) rows in stst.

Raglan shaping:
Cast off 3sts at the beginning of the next 2 rows.
Row 3. K1, slip 1, K1, psso, knit to last 3sts, K2 tog, K1.

Row 4. K1, purl to last st, K1.
Repeat Rows 3 and 4 until 10 (12, 14)sts remain. Cast off.

LEFT FRONT

Cast on 18 (20, 22)sts.
Row 1. (K1, P1) rib to last 4sts, K4.
Row 2. K4, * (K1, P1) rib; repeat from * to end of row.
Row 3. (K1, P1) rib to last 4sts, K4.
Row 4. (Make a buttonhole) K2, yfwd, K2 tog, * (K1, P1) rib; repeat from * to end of row.

Keeping the garter st border, work 1 (3, 3) rows in rib.

Next row. K4, rib 2 (1, 2), * increase in next st, rib 2 (3, 3); repeat from * twice, increase in next st, rib 2 (2, 3). (22, 24, 26sts)

Make a buttonhole on the 10th (12th, 12th) row from previous buttonhole and then 2 more on every following 9th (10th, 12th) row.

Keeping the garter st border, work 14 (14, 16) rows in stocking stitch.

Raglan and Neck shaping:

Row 1. Cast off 3sts, knit to end of row.

Row 2. K4, purl to last st, K1.

Row 3. K1, slip 1, K1, psso, knit to end of row.

Repeat Rows 2 and 3 until 12 (13, 14)sts remain, ending at neck edge.

Next row. Cast off 5 (6, 7)sts, purl to last st, K1.

Next row. K1, slip 1, K1, psso, knit to end of row.

Next row. P2 tog, purl to last st, K1.

Next row. K1, slip 1, K1, psso, K2.

Next row. P2 tog, P1, K1.

Next row. K1, slip 1, K1, psso.

Next row. P1, K1.

Next row. K2 tog. Fasten off.

RIGHT FRONT

Work as given for Left Front, omitting the buttonholes and working the garter st border at opposite end until raglan shaping is reached, ending with a knit row.

Raglan and Neck shaping:

Work as given for Left Front, omitting the buttonholes.

SLEEVES (BOTH ALIKE)

Cast on 20 (22, 24)sts.

Work 6 rows in garter st.

Change to stocking stitch and increase one st at each end of the 3rd and following 2nd (4th, 4th) row until there are 28 (30, 34)sts.

Continue without shaping until the sleeve measures 6.5cm (7, 7.5cm).

Raglan shaping:

Work as given for the back until 4sts remain. Cast off.

COLLAR

Stitch the sleeves into position.

Beginning at the centre of the band, pick up and knit 38 (42, 46)sts evenly all round neck.

Work 11 rows in garter st. Cast off.

To make up:

Join side and sleeve seams. Sew on buttons to correspond with buttonholes.

THE LEGGINGS

Work as for the first 3 sizes of GIRL'S OUTDOOR SET.

THE BERET

Cast on 56 (64, 72)sts.
Work 6 rows in (K1, P1) rib.
Next row. K3, * increase in next st, K6 (7, 8); repeat from * to last 4 (5, 6)sts, increase in next st, K3 (4, 5). (64, 72, 80sts)
Commencing with a purl row, work 9 (9, 11) rows in stocking stitch.

Shaping for Crown:
Next row. * K6, K2 tog; repeat from * to end of row.
Next and every alt row: Purl.
Next row. * K5, K2 tog; repeat from * to end of row.
Next row. * K4, K2 tog; repeat from * to end of row.
Continue to decrease in this fashion until (K2 tog) is worked all across row. Break off yarn and thread through remaining sts. Draw up tightly and join seam.

GIRL'S OUTDOOR SET

To fit dolls
30cm (35, 40, and 51cm)

MATERIALS:
Coat: 75g (75, 100, 125g) 8ply yarn
Leggings: 75g (75, 75, 100g) 8ply yarn
Bonnet: 25g 8ply yarn
pr 4.00mm knitting needles
70cm each of narrow and wide ribbon
45cm of elastic
3 buttons

THE COAT

BACK

Cast on 54 (60, 66, 78)sts.
Work 6 rows in garter st.

Continue in stocking stitch until work measures 10cm (11.5, 13, 14cm), ending with a purl row.
Next row. * K1, K2 tog; repeat from * to end of row. (36, 40, 44, 52sts)
Work 5 rows in garter st.
Work 4 rows in stocking stitch.

Raglan shaping:

Cast off 3sts at the beginning of the next 2 rows.
Row 3. K1, slip 1, K1, psso, knit to last 3sts, K2 tog, K1.
Row 4. K1, purl to last st, K1.
Repeat Rows 3 and 4 until 10 (12, 14, 18)sts remain. Cast off.

LEFT FRONT

Cast on 31 (34, 37, 43)sts.
Work 6 rows in garter st.
Next row. Knit.
Next row. K4, purl to end of row.
Repeat the last 2 rows until work measures 10cm (11.5, 13, 14cm), ending with a purl row.
Next row. * K1, K2 tog; repeat from * to last 4sts, K4. (22, 24, 26, 30sts)

Work 5 rows in garter st.

Keeping the garter st border, work 4 rows in stocking stitch.

Raglan and Neck shaping:

Row 1. Cast off 3sts, knit to end of row.
Row 2. K4, purl to last st, K1.
Row 3. K1, slip 1, K1, psso, knit to end of row.
Repeat Rows 2 and 3 until 12 (13, 14, 16)sts remain, ending at the neck edge.
Next row. Cast off 5 (6, 7, 9)sts, purl to last st, K1.
Next row. K1, slip 1, K1, psso, knit to end of row.
Next row. K2 tog, purl to last st, K1.
Next row. K1, slip 1, K1, psso, K2.
Next row. K2 tog, P1, K1.
Next row. K1, slip 1, K1, psso.
Next row. P1, K1.
Next row. K2 tog. Fasten off.

RIGHT FRONT

Work as given for Left Front (knitting 4sts at the end of every purl row for the border) until work measures 10cm (11.5, 13, 14cm), ending with a purl row.
Next row. K4, * K2 tog, K1; repeat from * to end of row. (22, 24, 26, 30sts)

Work 2 rows in garter st.
Next row. (Make a buttonhole) Knit to last 4sts, K2 tog, yfwd, K2.

Work 2 rows in garter st.

Keeping the garter st border, work 5 rows in stocking stitch.

Next row. Cast off 3sts, purl to last 4sts, K4.

Next row. Knit to last 3sts, K2 tog, K1.

Next row. K1, purl to last 4sts, K4.

Making another buttonhole in the 10th (10th, 12th, 14th) row from the previous buttonhole, repeat the last 2 rows until 13 (14, 15, 17)sts remain, ending at the front edge.

Next row. K2, yfwd, K2 tog, knit to last 3sts, K2 tog, K1.

Next row. K1, purl to last 4sts, K4.

Next row. Cast off 5 (6, 7, 9)sts, knit to last 3sts, K2 tog, K1.

Next row. K1, P4, K1.

Next row. K3, K2 tog, K1.

Next row. K1, P2, K2 tog.

Next row. K1, K2 tog, K1.

Next row. K1, P2 tog.

Next row. K2.

Next row. P2 tog. Fasten off.

SLEEVES (BOTH ALIKE)

Cast on 20 (22, 24, 34)sts.
Work 6 rows in garter st.

Change to stocking stitch and increase one st at each end of the 3rd and following 2nd (4th, 4th, 6th) row until there are 28 (30, 34, 38)sts.
Continue without shaping until the sleeve measures 6.5cm (7, 7.5, 9cm).

Raglan shaping:
Work as given for the back until 4sts remain. Cast off.

COLLAR

Stitch the sleeves into position. Beginning at the centre of the band, pick up and knit 38 (42, 46, 50)sts evenly all round neck.
Work 11 rows in garter st. Cast off.

To make up:
Join side and sleeve seams. Sew on the buttons to correspond with the buttonholes.

THE LEGGINGS

RIGHT LEG

Cast on 44 (48, 52, 60)sts.
Work 3 rows in (K1, P1) rib.

Next row. K2, * yfwd, K2 tog; repeat from * to end of row.
Work 4 rows in rib.

Change to stocking stitch and shape back as follows:
K6, turn, purl back.
K12, turn, purl back.
K18, turn, purl back.
K24, turn, purl back.
K30, turn, purl back.

Next row. Knit across all sts.
Continue in stocking stitch until the short edge measures 9cm (10.5, 11.5, 14cm).

Cast off 3sts at the beginning of the next 2 rows.

K2 tog at each end of next and every alt row until 22 (24, 26, 30)sts remain, ending with a purl row.

Work 4 rows in stocking stitch.

Next row. K1, * yfwd, K2 tog; repeat from * to last st, K1.

Next row. Purl.

Next row. K15 (16, 17, 19), turn.

Next row. P8, turn.

Work 4 (6, 8, 12) rows in stocking stitch. Break off yarn.

With right side facing and beginning near the sts on right-hand needle, pick up and knit 3 (4, 5, 7)sts up the side of the instep, K8, pick up and knit 3 (4, 5, 7)sts down the other side of the instep, knit 7 (8, 9, 11)sts on the left-hand needle.

(28, 32, 36, 44sts)

Next and every alt row: Purl.

Next row. K2 tog, K9 (11, 13, 17), K2 tog, K2, K2 tog, K9 (11, 13, 17), K2 tog.

Next row. K2 tog, K7 (9, 11, 15), K2 tog, K2, K2 tog, K7 (9, 11, 15), K2 tog.

Next row. K2 tog, K5 (7, 9, 13), K2 tog, K2, K2 tog, K5 (7, 9, 13), K2 tog.

Next row. (30cm doll only):
Cast off.

(35, 40 and 51cm dolls only): Purl.

Next row. K2 tog, K5 (7, 11), K2 tog, K2, K2 tog, K5 (7, 11), K2 tog. Cast off.

LEFT LEG

Work as given for Right Leg, reversing the back shaping by commencing P6, turn, knit back.

To make up:

Join each leg, then the front and back seams. Thread elastic through the holes at the waist, and ribbon through the holes at the ankles.

THE BONNET

Cast on 46 (50, 54, 62)sts.

Work 6 rows in garter st.

Change to stocking stitch and continue until work measures 6.5cm (7.5, 9, 11.5cm).

Decrease for Crown:

Next row. K2 tog, * K2, K2 tog; repeat from * to end of row.

Next and every alt row: Purl.

Next row. K1, * K1, K2 tog; repeat from * to end of row.

Next row. K1, * K2 tog; repeat from * to end of row.

Next row. K2 tog across row.

Draw thread through the remaining sts and draw up tightly.

To make up:

Stitch edges of Bonnet from crown to within 5cm of front edge. Sew on ribbons.

THE ROMPERS

MATERIALS:
50g (50, 75g) 8ply yarn
pr 4.00mm knitting needles
5 buttons

BACK
Cast on 8 (12, 16)sts.
Work in pattern as follows:
Rows 1 and 2. (K2, P2) to end of row.
Rows 3 and 4. (P2, K2) to end of row.
These 4 rows form the pattern.
Work 2 (2, 4) rows in pattern.

Cast on 4sts at the beginning of the next 4 rows, then 6sts at the beginning of the next 2 rows.
(36, 40, 44sts)
Work in pattern until side edge measures 5cm (6.5, 8cm).

Shape Back:
Next 2 rows. Pattern to the last 4 (6, 6)sts, turn.

Next 2 rows. Pattern to the last 8 (12, 12)sts, turn.
Next 2 rows. Pattern to the last 12 (16, 16)sts, turn.
Next row. Pattern to end of row.
Work 5 rows in (K1, P1) rib.

Divide for Back opening:
Next row. K18 (20, 22), turn.
Cast on 2sts.
Keeping 3sts at centre edge in garter st, work 3 (5, 7) rows in stocking stitch , beginning with a purl row.

Raglan shaping:
Cast off 4sts, knit to last 2sts, yfwd, K2 tog (buttonhole made).
Row 2. K3, purl to last st, K1.

Row 3. K1, slip 1, K1, psso, knit to end of row.
Repeat Rows 2 and 3 until 13 (14, 15)sts remain.
Make another buttonhole at the end of the next knit row, then continue with raglan shaping until 7 (8, 9)sts remain. Cast off.
Rejoin yarn to the remaining sts at the centre. Cast on 2sts.
Beginning with a knit row, and keeping the 3 centre sts in garter st, work 5 (7, 9) rows in stocking stitch.

Raglan shaping:
Cast off 4sts, purl to last 3sts, K3.
Row 2. Knit to last 3sts, K2 tog, K1.
Row 3. K1, purl to last 3sts, K3.
Repeat Rows 2 and 3 until 7 (8, 9)sts remain. Cast off.

FRONT
Cast on 8 (12, 16)sts.
Work 2 rows in pattern.
Row 3. (30cm doll)
P2 tog, yon, K2, P2, yon, K2 tog.
(35cm doll) P2, K1, yon, P2 tog, P1, K1, K2 tog, yon, P1, K2.
(40cm doll) P2, K2, yon, P2 tog, K2, P2, K2 tog, yon, P2 tog, K2.
Row 4. (P2, K2) to end of row.

Work as for Back, omitting shaping, until ribbing at waist is complete.

Work 4 (6, 8) rows in stocking stitch.

Raglan shaping:
Cast off 4sts at the beginning of the next 2 rows.
Row 3. K1, slip 1, K1, psso, knit to last 3sts, K2 tog, K1.
Row 4. K1, purl to last st, K1.
Repeat Rows 3 and 4 until 16 (18, 20)sts remain, ending with a purl row.

Neck shaping:
K1, slip 1, K1, psso, K3, cast off 4 (6, 8)sts, K3, K2 tog, K1.
Working on first group of sts, proceed as follows:
Row 1. K1, P3, K1.
Row 2. (K2 tog) twice, K1.
Row 3. K1, P2 tog.
Row 4. K2.
Row 5. P2 tog. Fasten off.

Rejoin yarn to the remaining sts at the neck edge.
Row 1. K1, P3, K1.
Row 2. K1, slip 1, K1, psso, K2 tog.
Row 3. P2 tog, K1.
Row 4. K2.
Row 5. P2 tog. Fasten off.

SLEEVES (BOTH ALIKE)
Cast on 30 (32, 34)sts.
Work 4 rows in (K1, P1) rib. Work 2 (2, 4) rows in stocking stitch.

Raglan shaping:
Work as given for Front until 4sts remain. Cast off.

NECK BAND

Stitch sleeves to the back and front along raglan shaping. With right side facing, pick up and knit 36 (40, 44)sts evenly all round the neck. Work 3 rows in (K1, P1) rib, making another buttonhole on the 2nd row. Cast off in rib.

To make up:

Join side and sleeve seams. Stitch down cast-on sts of back opening, placing right over left. Sew on buttons to correspond with buttonholes.

THE VEST
(not shown)

MATERIALS:

25g 8ply yarn
pr 4.00mm knitting needles

Cast on 32 (36, 40)sts and work 9cm (10.5, 12cm) in (K2, P2) rib.

Neck:

Rib 10 (11, 12), cast off 12 (14, 16)sts, rib 10 (11, 12) keeping the odd stitch in the medium size in knit.

Rib 5cm on first group of sts, ending at inside edge.
Break off yarn.

Rejoin yarn to second group of sts and work 5cm, ending at inside edge.
Cast on 12 (14, 16)sts and work across the first group of sts.
Work 9cm (10.5, 12cm) in rib, on all sts. Cast off in rib.

To make up:

Fold over work so that the cast-off edge is level with the cast-on edge. Stitch each side seam leaving sufficient room at the top for armholes.

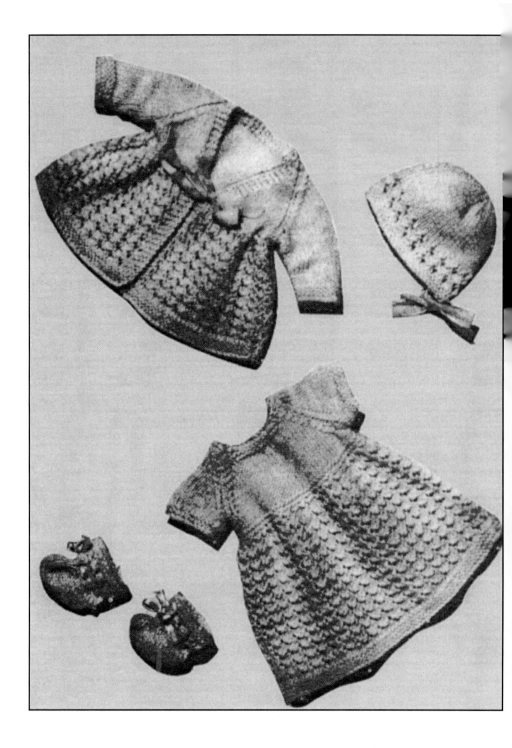

A DAINTILY PATTERNED OUTFIT

(shown opposite)

MATERIALS:

Dress: 50g (75, 100g) 8ply yarn
Matinee Jacket: 50g (50, 75g) 8ply yarn
Bonnet and Bootees: 25g 8ply yarn
pr 4.00mm knitting needles
70cm of narrow ribbon
1.4m of wide ribbon
3 buttons

THE DRESS

FRONT

Cast on 51 (57, 63)sts.
Work 6 rows in garter st.
Now work in pattern as follows:
Row 1. Knit.
Row 2. K1, purl to last st, K1.
Rows 3 and 4. * K1, yfwd, K2 tog;
repeat from * to end of row.

Repeat these 4 rows until the work
measures 13cm (14, 15cm), ending
with a Row 2.
Next row. * K1, K2 tog; repeat from
* to end of row. (34, 38, 42sts)
Work 3 rows in garter st (waist) and
4 rows in stocking stitch.

Raglan shaping:

Cast off 3sts at the beginning of the
next 2 rows.
Row 3. K1, slip 1, K1, psso, knit to
last 3sts, K2 tog, K1.
Row 4. K1, purl to last st, K1.

Repeat Rows 3 and 4 until 18 (20,
22)sts remain, ending with a Row 3.
Next row. K1, P4, K8 (10, 12), P4,
K1.
Next row. As Row 3.
Next row. K1, P2, K10 (12, 14), P2,
K1.
Next row. K1, slip 1, K1, psso, K3,
cast off 4 (6, 8)sts, K3, K2 tog, K1.
Next row. Knit.
Next row. (K2 tog) twice, K1.
Next row. K1, K2 tog.
Next row. Knit.
Next row. K2 tog. Fasten off.

Rejoin yarn to the remaining sts at
the neck edge.
Next row. Knit.
Next row. K1, slip 1, K1, psso,
K2 tog.
Next row. K2 tog, K1.
Next row. K2.
Next row. K2 tog. Fasten off.

BACK

Work as for Front until garter st rows
at the waist have been completed.

Divide for Back opening:

Next row. K17 (19, 21), turn, cast
on 2sts.

Next row. K3, purl to last st, K1. Keeping the 3 centre edge sts in garter st, work 2 rows in stocking st.

Raglan shaping:
Cast off 3sts, knit to end of row.
Row 2. K3, purl to last st, K1.
Row 3. K1, slip 1, K1, psso, knit to end.
Repeat Rows 2 and 3 until 13 (15, 17)sts remain, ending with a Row 2.
Next row. (Make a buttonhole) K1, slip 1, K1, psso, knit to last 2sts, yfwd, K2 tog.
Continue with raglan decreases until 9 (10, 11)sts remain, ending with a purl row.
Make another buttonhole in the next row.
Next row. Knit.
Work 1 more decrease row.
(7, 8, 9sts)
Next row. Knit.
Cast off.

Rejoin yarn to the remaining sts at the centre, cast on 2sts.

Omitting buttonholes, work to match the other half, ending raglan decrease rows with K2 tog, K1.

SLEEVES (BOTH ALIKE)
Cast on 22 (24, 26)sts.
Work 4 rows in garter st.
Row 5. K0 (1, 2), * increase in next st, K3; repeat from * 5 times, increase in next st, K1 (2, 3). (28, 30, 32sts)

Beginning with a purl row, work 2 rows in stocking stitch.

Raglan shaping:
Work as given for Front until 6sts remain, ending with a knit row.
Next row. Knit.
Next row. K1, slip 1, K1, psso, K2 tog, K1.
Next row. Knit. Cast off.

To make up:
Stitch side and sleeve seams. Stitch sleeves into position. Sew on the buttons to correspond with the buttonholes.

THE MATINEE JACKET

BACK
Cast on 51 (57, 63)sts.
Work 6 rows in garter st.
Work in pattern as given for Front of Dress until work measures 7.5cm (9, 10.5cm), ending with a wrong side row.
Next row. (right side facing) (K1, K2 tog) repeat to end of row.
Next row. Knit.
Next row. K2, * yfwd, K2 tog, K2; repeat from * to end of row.
Next row. Knit.
Work 4 rows in stocking stitch.

Raglan shaping:
Work as given for Front of Dress until 10 (12, 14)sts remain. Cast off.

LEFT FRONT
Cast on 28 (31, 34)sts.
Work 6 rows in garter st.
Now work in pattern as follows:
Row 1. Knit.
Row 2. K4, purl to end of row.
Row 3. * K1, yfwd, K2 tog; repeat from * to last 4sts, K4.
Row 4. K4, * K1, yfwd, K2 tog; repeat from * to end of row.
Repeat last 4 rows until work measures 7.5cm (9, 10.5cm), ending with a wrong side row.
Next row. * K1, K2 tog; repeat from * to last 4sts, K4. (20, 22, 24sts)
Next row. Knit.
Next row. K2 (4, 2), * yfwd, K2 tog, K2; repeat from * to last 2sts, K2.
Next row. Knit.
Keeping the garter st border, work 2 rows in stocking stitch.
Next row. Knit to last 6sts, K2 tog, K4.
Next row. K4, purl to end.
Next row. Cast off 3sts, knit to last 4sts, K4.
Next row. K4, purl to last st, K1.
Next row. K1, slip 1, K1, psso, knit to last 6sts, K2 tog, K4.
Next row. K4, purl to last st, K1.
Next row. K1, slip 1, K1, psso, knit to end of row.
Next row. K4, purl to last st, K1.
Repeat the last 4 rows until 6sts remain.
Next row. K4, P1, K1.
Next row. K1, K2 tog, K3.

Next row. K5.
Next row. K1, K2 tog, K2.
Work 15 rows in garter st.
Cast off.

RIGHT FRONT
Work as given for Left Front reversing all shapings and working in pattern as follows:
Row 1. Knit.
Row 2. Purl to last 4sts, K4.
Row 3. K4, * K1, yfwd, K2 tog; repeat from * to end of row.
Row 4. * K1, yfwd, K2 tog; repeat from * to last 4 sts, K4.

SLEEVES (BOTH ALIKE)
Cast on 20 (22, 24)sts and work 4 (4, 6) rows in garter st.
Change to stocking stitch and increase one st at each end of the 3rd and every following 3rd (4th, 4th) rows until there are 28 (30, 32)sts. Work until sleeve measures 6.5cm (7, 7.5cm).

Raglan shaping:
Work as given for Front of Dress until 4sts remain. Cast off.

To make up:
Join side and sleeve seams. Join ends of borders and stitch to back of neck. Thread ribbon through ribbon holes at waist.

THE BONNET

Cast on 48 (51, 54)sts.
Work 4 rows in garter st.

Now work in pattern as follows:
Row 1. Knit.
Row 2. K1, purl to last st, K1.
Rows 3 and 4. * K1, yfwd, K2 tog;
repeat from * to end of row.

Repeat these 4 rows once more.
Next row. Knit (decreasing one st
at each end of row for small size and
one st at the beginning of row for
medium size). (46, 50, 54sts)

Beginning with a purl row, continue
in stocking stitch until work measures
6.5cm (7.5, 9cm).

Decrease for Crown:
Row 1. K2 tog, * K2, K2 tog; repeat
from * to end of row.
Row 2 and alt rows: Purl.
Row 3. K1, * K1, K2 tog; repeat
from * to end of row.
Row 5. K1, * K2 tog; repeat from *
to end of row.
Row 7. K2 tog all along row.
Row 8. Purl.
Thread yarn through the remaining
sts and draw up tight.

To make up:
Stitch edges together from crown to
within 5cm of front edge. Sew on
ribbons.

THE BOOTEES (make 2)

Cast on 21 (24, 27)sts.
Work 4 rows in garter st.
Work 4 rows of pattern as given for
The Bonnet. Work 2 rows in stst.
Next row. (K1, yfwd, K2 tog) repeat
to end of row.
Next row. Purl.
Next row. K14 (16, 18), turn.
Next row. P7 (8, 9), turn.
Work 4 (6, 8) rows on these sts.
Break off yarn. Right side facing,
pick up and K3 (4, 5)sts up the first
side of instep, K7 (8, 9)sts of instep
and then pick up and K3 (4, 5)sts
down other side of instep, knit sts on
left-hand needle. (27, 32, 37sts)
Next and every alt row: Purl.
Next row. K2 tog, K9 (11, 13)
K2 tog, K1 (2, 3), K2 tog, K9 (11,
13), K2 tog.
Next row. K2 tog, K7 (9, 11),
K2 tog, K1 (2, 3), K2 tog, K7 (9, 11),
K2 tog.
Next row. K2 tog, K5 (7, 9),
K2 tog, K1 (2, 3), K2 tog, K5 (7, 9),
K2 tog.
Next row. (30cm size only): Cast off.

(35 and 40cm sizes): Purl.
Next row. K2 tog, K5 (7), K2 tog,
K2 (3), K2 tog, K5 (7), K2 tog.
Cast off.

To make up:
Join leg and base of foot of each
bootee. Thread ribbon through
ribbonholes at ankle.

CAPE FOR GOING PLACES

MATERIALS:
75g (100, l00g) 8ply yarn
pr 4.00mm knitting needles
70cm of 10mm wide ribbon
2 buttons

Cast on 117 (125, 133)sts and work 8 rows in garter st, then work in pattern as follows:

Row 1. K6, yfwd, K2 tog, K5, * yfwd, slip 1, K2 tog, psso, yfwd, K5; repeat from * to last 8sts, yfwd, slip 1, K1, psso, K6.

Row 2 and every alt row. K5, purl to last 5sts, K5.

Row 3. K6, * K1, yfwd, slip 1, K1, psso, K3, K2 tog, yfwd; repeat from * to last 7sts, K7.

Row 5. K6, * K2, yfwd, slip 1, K1, psso, K1, K2 tog, yfwd, K1; repeat from * to last 7sts, K7.

Row 7. K6, * K3, yfwd, slip 1, K2 tog, psso, yfwd, K2; repeat from * to last 7sts, K7.

Row 8. K5, purl to last 5sts, K5.

These 8 rows form the pattern, repeat them until there are 7 (8, 9) complete patterns.

Shape yoke:

Row 1. K2, yfwd, K2 tog, K1, * K2 tog, K2; repeat from * to last 8sts, K2 tog, K6. (90, 96, 102sts)

Row 2. K5, * K1, P1; repeat from * to last 5sts, K5.

Repeat last row 6 more times.

Next row. K2, yfwd, K2 tog, K2, P1, * K2 tog, P2 tog, K1, P1; repeat from * to last 5sts, K5.
(64, 68, 72sts)

Work in rib for 7 rows, keeping 5sts at each end in garter st.

Next row. K6, * P2 tog, K2 tog, rib 4; repeat from * to last 10 (6, 10)sts

1ˢᵗ size only: P2 tog, K2 tog, P1, K5.
2ⁿᵈ size only: K2 tog, K4.
3ʳᵈ size only: P2 tog, K2 tog, P1, K5.
(50, 53, 56sts)
Next row. K5, rib to last 5sts, K5.
Next row. (make ribbonholes) K1,
* K1, yfwd, K2 tog; repeat from * to
last st, K1.
Next row. K5, purl to last 5sts, K5.
Next row. Cast off 6sts, knit to end
of row.
Next row. Cast off 6sts, K5 including
the st on needle, purl to last 5sts,
K5.

Next row. K15 (16, 17), increase in
each of the next 8 (9, 10)sts, knit to
end of row. (46, 50, 54sts)
Next row. K5, purl to last 5sts, K5.
Next row. Knit.
Repeat these last 2 rows until the
hood measures 10cm (11.5, 13cm)
from the ribbonholes. Cast off.

To make up:
Join the hood across the top. Thread
the ribbon through the ribbonholes
and sew on buttons to correspond
with buttonholes.

BUSTER'S OUTFIT

MATERIALS:
Underpants and Jumper:
25g (50, 75g) light colour
8ply yarn
Trousers and Cap:
50g (50, 75g) dark colour,
small quantity light colour
8ply yarn
pr 4.00mm knitting needles
45cm of elastic
4 buttons

THE UNDERPANTS

Cast on 28 (32, 36)sts.
Work 4 rows in stocking stitch.
Row 5. (right side facing) Purl.
Continue in stst (beginning with a purl row), until work measures 5cm (6, 6.5cm) from the purl row.

Leg shaping:
K2 tog at each end of every row until 6sts remain.
Work on these sts for 3 (5, 5) rows, ending with a purl row.
Increase one st at each end of every row until there are 28 (32, 36)sts on the needle.
Work 5cm (6, 6.5cm) in stst.
Purl a row on the right side of work and stst 4 more rows. Cast off.

To make up:
Join side seams. Fold over hem to wrong side on purl row and hem. Thread elastic through hem.

THE JUMPER

FRONT
Cast on 34 (38, 42)sts and work 6 (8, 8) rows in (K1, P1) rib.
Change to stst and work 10 (12, 14) rows.

Raglan shaping:
Cast off 3sts at the beginning of next 2 rows.

Row 3. K1, slip 1, K1, psso, knit to last 3sts, K2 tog, K1.
Row 4. K1, purl to last st, K1.
Repeat Rows 3 and 4 until 16 (18, 20)sts remain, ending with a Row 4.

Neck shaping:
Next row. K1, slip 1, K1, psso, K3, cast off 4 (6, 8)sts, K3, K2 tog, K1.
Now work on the first group of sts.
Row 1. K1, P3, K1.
Row 2. (K2 tog) twice, K1.
Row 3. K1, P2 tog.
Row 4. K2.
Row 5. P2 tog. Fasten off.

Rejoin yarn at the neck edge to the remaining sts.
Row 1. K1, P3, K1.
Row 2. K1, slip 1, K1, psso, K2 tog.
Row 3. P2 tog, K1.
Row 4. K2.
Row 5. P2 tog. Fasten off.

BACK
Work as given for the front until 8 (10, 12) rows of stocking stitch have been worked.
Next row. K17 (19, 21), turn.
Cast on 2sts.
Next row. K3, purl to end of row.

Keeping the centre sts in garter st, work as follows:
Raglan shaping:
Row 1. Cast off 3sts, knit to end of row.

Row 2. K3, purl to last st, K1.
Row 3. K1, slip 1, K1, psso, knit to end of row.
Repeat last 2 rows until 7 (8, 9)sts remain, ending with a purl row.
Cast off.

Rejoin yarn to the remaining sts at the centre. Cast on 2sts.
Next row. Knit.

Raglan shaping:
Row 1. Cast off 3sts, purl to last 3sts, K3.
Row 2. Knit to last 3sts, K2 tog, K1.
Row 3. K1, purl to last 3sts, K3.

Repeat last 2 rows until 14 (15, 16)sts remain, ending with a purl row.
Next row. (Make a buttonhole) K1, slip 1, yfwd, K2 tog, knit to last 3sts, K2 tog, K1.
Repeat Rows 2 and 3 until 7 (8, 9)sts remain, ending with a purl row.
Cast off.

SLEEVES (BOTH ALIKE)
Cast on 20 (22, 24)sts and work 4 (4, 6) rows in (K1, P1) rib.
Change to stst and increase one st at each end of the 3rd and every following 3rd (3rd, 4th) row until there are 28 (30, 32)sts.

Continue until the work measures 6cm (7, 8cm).

Raglan shaping:
Work as given for the front until 4sts remain. Cast off.

NECK BAND
Stitch the sleeves to the back and front along raglan shaping, pick up and knit 36 (40, 44)sts evenly all round neck.
Work 3 rows in (K1, P1) rib, making another buttonhole above the first one on the 2nd row. Cast off in rib.

To make up:
Join side and sleeve seam. Stitch down cast-on edges of back opening. Sew on buttons to correspond with buttonholes.

THE TROUSERS

RIGHT LEG
Cast on 36 (40, 44)sts in dark yarn.
Work 6 (6, 8) rows in (K1, P1) rib.

Back shaping:
K6, turn, purl back.
K12, turn, purl back.
K18, turn, purl back.
K24, turn, purl back.
Knit across all sts.
Continue in stocking stitch until the short edge measures 7cm (8, 9cm), ending with a purl row.
Increase one st at each end of the next and every alt row until there are 44 (48, 52)sts, ending with a purl row.

Now work 3 (5, 5) rows in garter st. Cast off.

LEFT LEG

Work as given for Right Leg, shaping back as follows:

P6, turn, knit back.
P12, turn, knit back.
P18, turn, knit back.
P24, turn, knit back.
Purl across all sts.

SHOULDER STRAPS

Cast on 6sts.
Row 1. K2, (P1, K1) twice.
Repeat this row until the strap measures 15cm (16.5, 18cm).
Next row. (Make a buttonhole) K2, cast off 2sts, rib 2.
Next row. K2, cast on 2sts, rib 2.
Cast off.
Work another strap to correspond.

To make up:

Join front and back seams, then the leg seam. Stitch one end of each strap to the waist on the back of the trousers placing them 2.5cm from the centre seam. Sew 2 buttons on front waist band of trousers.

THE CAP

Cast on 48 (56, 64)sts in dark yarn and work 6 rows in (K1, P1) rib.

Work in stocking stitch as follows:
4 rows dark colour.
6 rows light colour.
4 rows dark colour.
4 rows light colour.
2 rows dark colour.
2 rows light colour.

Change to dark colour.
Work 4 rows.
Next row. (K6, K2 tog) to end of row.
Work 7 rows without shaping.
Next row. (K5, K2 tog) to end of row.
Work 7 rows without shaping.
Next row. (K4, K2 tog) to end of row.
Work 7 rows without shaping.
Next row. (K2 tog) to end.

Break off yarn and thread through remaining sts. Draw up tightly and join seam. Using dark and light yarn, make a pom-pom (see Page 22), and attach to top of cap. Turn up lower edge of cap.

TO MAKE A POM-POM

Using the pattern shown, cut two circles from cardboard (or craft plastic). Cut out and discard the centre circles. Using desired colour, thread the yarn around the two circles until the centre hole has been filled. Cut the yarn between the two circles of cardboard, sliding the scissors between the two circles. Using double yarn, tie around (between the circles) and secure. Remove the circles. Trim the pom-pom, leaving the tying yarn to secure the pom-pom to the cap.

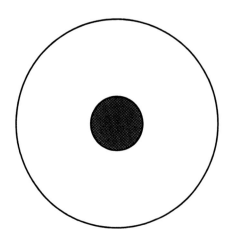

These books are also available (by Vicki Moodie, unless shown otherwise)

BK02	Hooked on Lace
BK03	Needles and Lace
BK04	Top that Towel
BK05	Laced with Love
BK06	More Towel Tops
BK07	Novelties in Lace
BK08	Paragon of Lace
BK09	Keep it Cosy
BK10	Basics in Lace
BK11	Knitted Coat-hanger Covers
BK12	Towel Tops & Motifs
BK13	Simple Jug Covers
BK14	More Knitted Lace
BK15	Easy Crocheted Bootees
BK16	Kitchen Towels
BK17	Doilies for my Daughter
BK18	Baby's Crocheted Rugs and Shawls
BK19	Crocheted Matinee Jackets
BK20	Baby's Knitted Rugs and Shawls
BK21	More Jug Covers
BK22	Crocheted Three Piece Sets
BK23	Occasional Lace
BK24	Crocheted Outfits for Dolls and Prem Babies
BK25	Doilies to crochet in 4ply cotton
BK26	Knitted Outfits for Dolls and Prem Babies (by Denny Kelly)
BK27	More Knitted Outfits for Dolls and Prem Babies
BK28	A Crocheted Library of Bookmarks
BK29	Hairpin Crochet Made Easy (by Betty Franks)
BK30	Animal Towel Tops and More
BK31	Favourite Knitted Outfits for Dolls and Prems
BK32	Showtime Tea Cosies
BK33	Crocheted Novelty Dressing Table Sets
BK34 (A4)	Crocheted Baby Shawls Round and Rectangle
BK35 (A4)	More Crocheted Shawls for Baby
BK36 (A4)	Crocheted Bags for Beginners
BK37 (A4)	Crocheted Coathanger Covers Book 1
BK38 (A4)	Stylish Jug Covers
BK39 (A4)	Distinctive Jug Covers to Crochet
BK40 (A4)	Crocheted Baby Outfits - Newborn to 9 months
BK41 (A4)	Dream Catchers and More to Crochet
BK42 (A4)	Four More Crocheted Dressing Table Sets
BK43 (A4)	Crocheted Doilies using Broomstick, Bavarian & Daisy Wheel
BK44 (A4)	Inspirational Tea Cosies knitted and crocheted
BKAG01	Sculptured Candlewicking (by Anne Green)
BKAG02	Australiana Candlewicking (by Anne Green)

The following Paragon knitting books are also available